D0010529

St. Lawrence Beluga

. . . .

ISBN 0-920775-86-1

OWL and the OWL colophon are trademarks of the Young Naturalist Foundation. Greey de Pencier Books is a licensed user of these trademarks.

Printed in Canada on recycled paper

A B C D E F

For permission to use copyrighted photos we thank: Jeff Foott, pp.4/5, 16/17, 30/31; Flip Nicklin, pp.10, 24; Tom McHugh / Photo Researchers Inc., p.13; Jeff Foott/DRK Photo, p.14; John Foster/Masterfile, p.14; Animals Animals/Richard Kolar, p.19; Bill Brooks/Masterfile, pp.21, 25; Barrett & MacKay/Masterfile, pp.26/27; Animals Animals/Ken Cole, p.26; Gordon R. Williamson/Bruce Coleman Inc., p.27; Sandy MacDonald, p.31; Hans Blohm/Masterfile, pp.28/29; Ron & Valerie Taylor/Bruce Coleman Inc., p.29.

We are grateful to Dr. Pierre Béland, St. Lawrence Institute of Ecotoxicology and Leone Pippard, President & Executive Director, Canadian Ecology Advocates, for their assistance in the preparation of this book.

Design by Word & Image Design Studio, Toronto

Silhouette illustrations by Dave McKay

Research by Katherine Farris

Cover photo by J.A. Kraulis/Masterfile

CANADA'S
ENDANGERED
ANiMALS

St. Lawrence Beluga

From OWL Magazine

Written by Sylvia Funston
Illustrated by Olena Kassian

OWL

Greey de Pencier Books

Introduction

Scientists describe certain animals as endangered to warn people that, unless we take special care, they will disappear forever from the world.

Many animals are endangered because people have taken over their wilderness homes. Others become endangered because they are over-hunted. Still others are endangered because pollution is poisoning them.

In this book you will discover how St. Lawrence belugas live. You will explore the special reasons they are endangered and find out what is being done — as well as what you can do — to help them survive far into the future.

Put on your thinking cap and discover how much you already know about beluga whales. *Answers page 32*

1. Belugas make many unusual noises. Which one of these would a beluga *not* make?
a. a sound like a police siren
b. a sound like a rusty hinge
c. a sound like a grunting pig

2. The bump on the front of a beluga's head is called a melon. What is inside it?
a. oil
b. air
c. water

3. Young belugas are called:
a. pups
b. chicks
c. calves.

A Baby Is Born

Something very special happens each summer
in the upper waters of the St. Lawrence River.
In shallow bays along the edges of
islands, beluga calves are born.

4. What are two favorite beluga games?
a. balancing stones on their heads
b. chasing the beluga that has the seaweed
c. hide and seek

5. What color is a baby beluga when it is born?
a. white with pink spots
b. grayish brown
c. brown with white spots

6. Belugas are the only whales that:
a. turn their heads to look around
b. make noises through their blowholes
c. have a thick layer of blubber.

7. A mother beluga uses her beak to:
a. defend her baby
b. bump her baby to make it behave
c. "rub noses" with her mate.

Belugas do not develop their mermaid-shaped tales until they are fully grown.

Next to each mother swims an "aunt" beluga. She is ready to push the grayish-brown calf up to the surface for its first gulp of air. "Aunties" also often act as babysitters.

Baby Belugas

For two years a beluga calf drinks its mother's rich, creamy milk. When it is hungry, it nudges its mother close to one of her nipples and she squirts milk into its mouth.

Beluga calves love to play with stones and seaweed.

A beluga calf swims so close to its mother's back that it looks as if it is having a piggyback ride. As the mother's huge body cuts through the water it creates a current that pulls the calf along. By "surfing" in this way, the calf can keep up with the herd without getting too tired.

Feeding Time

A grown beluga usually eats two large meals and a couple of snacks a day. It eats many kinds of fish, worms and soft shellfish, and even plants. Because it cannot chew its food, it never eats anything with a hard shell. A beluga calf eats soft worms and shrimps that it finds in the mud on the river bottom.

By the time a beluga is five years old, it has learned how to hunt with the herd. At a signal from the lead whale, the huge white whales all dive together as if they were one large hunter.

A beluga calf grows its teeth at two years of age.

Humming Belugas

On the surface, belugas "talk" through their blowholes. Underwater, they close their blowholes and "hum" to each other. Belugas make another type of sound that is similar to the clicks that bats make when they hunt in the dark.

The clicking noises that belugas send out bounce off objects in the water and return to them as echoes. By listening for these echoes, belugas can locate things without being able to see them.

A beluga's blow hole is on the top of its head.

Noisy Belugas

So far, scientists have counted at least 200 different beluga sounds. Amazingly, a beluga can send out clicks, listen for their echoes to decide if there is any food or danger nearby *and* hold a conversation with another beluga, all at the same time!

St. Lawrence Belugas Are Amazing

▶ A beluga makes clicking sounds by rapidly moving air through a maze of tubes inside its head.

▶ A beluga listens for echoes from its clicking sounds with its entire head. Sound travels to its ears through its jaw bones and the oil-filled bump, or melon, on top of its head.

▶ By using muscles to flatten or pull up its melon, a beluga can fine tune the sounds it sends out into the water.

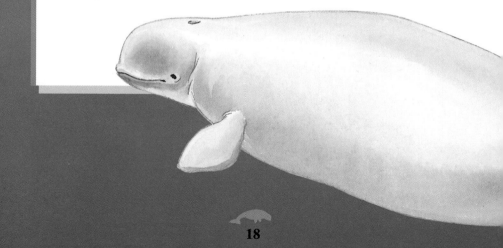

18

► It is not unusual to hear belugas chirp like birds, scream, snore or burp like people, grunt or moo like barnyard animals, yap like dogs or mew like cats.

► A fully grown beluga is slightly longer than a minivan and as heavy as $1\frac{1}{2}$ small cars.

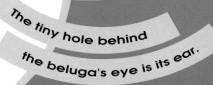

The tiny hole behind the beluga's eye is its ear.

Where Do Belugas Live?

Arctic belugas live in the cold waters at the top of the world. The endangered St. Lawrence belugas, however, live only in the St. Lawrence River.

Many thousands of years ago belugas lived in an ice-cold sea that covered Quebec and Ontario. When the sea slowly drained away, it left behind the St. Lawrence River.

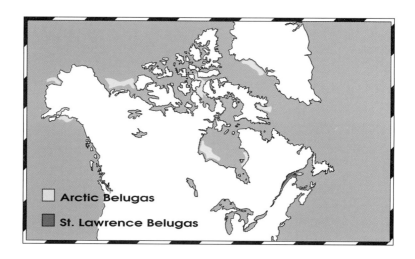

☐ Arctic Belugas

■ St. Lawrence Belugas

The north shore of the St. Lawrence River

The belugas stayed in the river because it is fed by a cold current from the Atlantic Ocean. This cold water is rich in tiny sea plants and animals that attract fish for belugas to eat. The river also offers many safe places for beluga calves.

The Beluga Up Close

▶ Fat lips allow the beluga to suck food out of the mud like a vacuum cleaner.

▶ The beluga's peg-like teeth are perfect for grabbing hold of fish, but no good for chewing.

▶ The older a beluga gets, the more curled up its flippers become.

▶ The beluga's crescent-shaped blowhole is surrounded by muscles that alter its shape, like a pair of lips, to make sounds.

▶ The thick layer of fatty blubber beneath the beluga's skin acts like a diver's wet suit to keep it warm.

▶ Sometimes the beluga's blubber keeps it too warm. Then the whale gets rid of body heat through its thin tail and flippers.

Up and Down the River

Each spring belugas follow large schools of fish up the St. Lawrence River.

In summer, young males and females group together. They travel quickly and hunt for fish in deep, cold water.

Females with young are found farther up river where the water is warmer. They travel slowly so their calves can keep up.

By late autumn the belugas head downriver towards the Gulf of St. Lawrence. They look for places where strong currents keep the water ice-free and where fish collect for winter.

Each season finds belugas in different parts of the river.

Québec

St. Lawrence Estuary

Saguenay R.

Summer
Spring, Summer, Autumn
Winter
All Seasons

Who Shares the River?

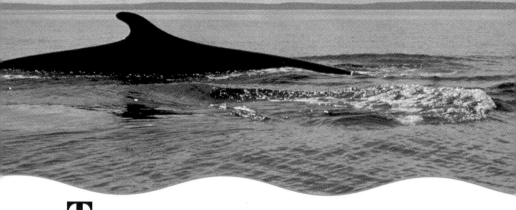

The endless supply of tiny plants and animals that flows into the river on its cold current makes the St. Lawrence a rich hunting ground for many animals.

A harp seal and her pup

Belugas share the icy St. Lawrence River in winter with harbor seals, gray seals and harp seals. They too feed on the fish that live in the river year round.

Plenty of food attracts fin whales (above) and minke whales to the river.

After the ice breaks in the spring, pods of minke and fin whales begin to arrive. They are followed by humpback and blue whales, harbor porpoise and white-sided dolphin.

In autumn the visiting whales head out to the ocean, once again leaving the river to the belugas and seals.

Why Are Belugas Endangered?

Disappearing Homes

When people dam a river, build bridges across it or dig deep-water ports for ships, they affect the animals in the river. If a shallow area where fish lay their eggs is lost, both the fish and the belugas that feed on them are affected.

Heavy river traffic can cause problems for belugas.

A school of herring swims upriver.

Poisonous Food

Worms, shrimps and fish eat poisons in the St. Lawrence River from factories along its banks and from chemicals that are used to fertilize crops and to kill farm pests. Because belugas eat so many worms, shrimps and fish, they become very badly poisoned.

What's Being Done?

Early in 1990 a decision was made to try to save the belugas by creating an underwater park where the Saguenay River meets the St. Lawrence.

This marine park will protect many of the places where belugas give birth or feed. People will not be allowed to dump garbage into the water or dredge the river bottom to make it deeper. Boating will be controlled and people will have to take great care when they build harbors or bridges. Owners of factories must also help by reducing the amount of pollution that enters the river.

The meeting point of

the Saguenay and

St. Lawrence Rivers

What Can You Do?

► Find out as much as possible about all endangered species and what is being done to help them. Then tell others what you have learned. Try these sources:

1. Your school and public libraries.

2. Canadian Wildlife Federation, 2740 Queensview Drive, Ottawa, ON K2B 1A2.

3. Federal Minister of the Environment, Terrasse de la Chaudière, 28th Floor, 10 Wellington St., Hull, P.Q. K1A 0H3 (Ask about belugas and reducing pollution.)

4. St. Lawrence National Institute of Ecotoxicology, 3872 Parc la Fontaine, Montréal, P.Q. H2L 3M6

► Get involved in helping the environment. Take part in OWL and *Chickadee* Magazines' HOOT Club Awards Program. Write to OWL Magazine, 56 The Esplanade, Suite 306, Toronto, ON M5E 1A7.

Answers to Quiz
1-a, 2-a, 3-c, 4-a and b, 5-b, 6-a, 7-b